Scholastic   5/09

W9-BIC-223

R.L.   P.V.
5.7   0.5

WEASELS

Amy-Jane Beer

Grolier
an imprint of
SCHOLASTIC
www.scholastic.com/librarypublishing

Published 2008 by Grolier
An imprint of Scholastic Library Publishing
Old Sherman Turnpike, Danbury,
Connecticut 06816

For The Brown Reference Group plc
Project Editor: Jolyon Goddard
Copy-editors: Lesley Ellis, Lisa Hughes,
    Wendy Horobin
Picture Researcher: Clare Newman
Designers: Jeni Child, Lynne Ross,
    Sarah Williams
Managing Editor: Bridget Giles

Volume ISBN-13: 978-0-7172-6263-2
Volume ISBN-10: 0-7172-6263-4

Nature's children. Set 2.
    p. cm.
  Includes bibliographical references and
  index.
  ISBN-13: 978-0-7172-8081-0
  ISBN-10: 0-7172-8081-0
  1. Animals--Encyclopedias, Juvenile. 1.
  Grolier (Firm)
  QL49.N383 2007
  590--dc22
                        2007026928

Printed and bound in China

PICTURE CREDITS

Front Cover: **Nature PL**: Aflo.

Back Cover: **Nature PL**: Gertrud and
Helmut Denzau; **NHPA**: Manfred Danegger,
Danny Green; **Photolibrary.com**: Les
Stocker.

Ardea: Ian Beams 2–3, 29, 34, Elizabeth
Bomford 38; **Corbis**: Markus Botzek/zefa 45,
Terry Whittaker/FLPA 5; **FLPA**: R. and M. Van
Nostrand 17; **Nature PL**: Arlo 33, Gertrude
and Helmut Denzau 41, Martin H. Smith 6,
Xi Zhinong 21; **Photolibrary.com**: Judd
Coone 10, Er Degginger 30, Juniors
Bildarchiv 14, Les Stocker 37; **Shutterstock**:
Ronnie Howard 22, Brian Sallee 9; **Still
Pictures**: G. Delpho/Wildlife 42, F. Hecker 4,
13, Thomas D. Mangelsen 46,
D. Tipling/Wildlife 18; **Superstock**:
Age Fotostock 26–27.

Contents

FACT FILE: Weasels

Class	Mammals (Mammalia)
Order	Carnivores (Carnivora)
Family	Weasels, mink, and polecats (Mustelidae)
Genus	*Mustela*
Species	Least weasel (*Mustela nivalis*), ermine or stoat (*Mustela erminea*), and long-tailed weasel (*Mustela frenata*)
World distribution	North and South America, Africa, and Eurasia
Habitat	Varied—meadows and pastures, woodland, farmland, tundra, and mountains
Distinctive physical characteristics	Long slim body, short legs, short pointed face; fur usually brown with pale markings
Habits	Solitary, active all year from dusk to dawn, stores excess food
Diet	Meat, usually rodents, rabbits, insects, lizards, or frogs

Introduction

Would you be offended if someone called you a
weasel? You probably would, because for some
reason, the word is often used to mean a sneaky
person, or someone who can't be trusted. But
actually weasels are smart, and work very
hard. They are also incredibly quick and agile.
Perhaps being a weasel isn't so bad after all.

**A weasel carefully
surveys an area for
its next meal.**

Weasels may be
small but they
can attack much
bigger prey, such
as rabbits.

A Bad Name

Weasels have a bad reputation for the same reason as many other wild animals, such as foxes, wolves, and birds of **prey**. Weasels are hunters, and sometimes they hunt the animals that humans want for themselves. In the past, people depended on the animals they raised for food and other products. Wild **predators**, even small ones like weasels, could cause big problems for domestic animals. Weasels love eggs. They also kill and eat animals such as chickens and rabbits. No matter what farmers do to try to stop them, these clever, skillful animals find a way to continue raiding farms for eggs and livestock. Because of the trouble they often caused, perhaps it's understandable that they were once considered pests.

Small, But Deadly

Weasels grow to between 5 and 16 inches (13–40 cm) long from their nose to the tip of their tail and weigh between 1 and 12 ounces (30–360 g) as adults. They are the smallest members of a family of **mammals** called mustelids. Other mustelids include otters, ferrets, fishers, mink, badgers, and wolverines. They are all cousins of weasels. The biggest of all the mustelids is the wolverine, which can weigh as much as 66 pounds (30 kg).

What all mustelids have in common is a long slim body and short legs. They are all also deadly predators, or hunters, with amazing speed, strength, and ferocity for their size.

A weasel finds a
rocky hiding place.

9

Weasels live in
most regions
of North and
South America.

Weasels of America

North America has three different types, or species, of weasels. They include the least weasel, the ermine or **stoat**, and the long-tailed weasel. There are two other species of weasels in South America. They are called the Amazon weasel and the Colombian weasel.

Paleontologists, or scientists who study **fossils**, think that weasels first appeared in Europe about 40 million years ago. They were very successful from the start and quickly spread throughout Asia, too.

About 25 million years ago, Asia and North America were joined. The two continents were connected at the place where the narrow strip of sea called the Bering Strait is now. So weasels arrived in North America by journeying overland from Asia.

Least Weasels

The smallest weasel in the world is called the least weasel and it lives in North America. It is found in many other places, too. It lives everywhere from the British Isles to North Africa, from Europe to Asia. Least weasels are about 6 to 8 inches (15–20 cm) long, and only about 2 inches (4 cm) of that is tail. Their small size and short tail are the easiest way to tell them apart from other weasels.

Least weasels are among the most successful predators in the whole world! They are the chief predator of mice and voles. They kill more mice and voles than any other animal. Small size is the secret of their success—they are so tiny that they can chase the mice right into their **burrows**, something very few other predators are small enough to do.

The small size of a least weasel helps it hide in the undergrowth.

13

Ermine keep the black tuft on their tail, even when they grow their white winter coat.

Ermine Everywhere

The ermine is another weasel that is found all over the world. It is a successful species. Like the least weasel, it is found in Europe and Asia, too, but there it is known by other names. In the United Kingdom it is usually called a stoat. Ermine is the old English name that the Pilgrims took with them to America. Back then, ermine were very unpopular animals. The European settlers must have been very disappointed to discover upon arriving in the Americas that one of their least-favorite chicken thieves was already there!

The ermine is bigger than the least weasel. It is about 10 to 14 inches (25–35 cm) long. But the most distinctive thing about the ermine is its tail, which has a black tuft at the end.

Long-tailed Weasel

Not surprisingly, the long-tailed weasel has the longest tail of all. Its tail measures a little more than half as long as the rest of its body, but with no black tuft like the ermine's. Sometimes the tail can be 10 inches (25 cm) long! The long-tailed weasel is the most common weasel in the United States. It can be found in almost all habitats from the Canadian border to Mexico. It is sometimes known as the bridled weasel because in some places it has white markings on its face that look like a horse's bridle.

However, telling weasels apart is all about the tails: short for the least weasel, long for the long-tailed weasel, and with a black tuft for the ermine.

Long-tailed weasels living in southern regions of North America may have pale markings on their face.

This weasel searches
for prey in a hollow log.

18

Home Ground

With their long, slim body and short legs, weasels can fit into very small spaces. They use all sorts of small nooks and crannies as homes. A weasel's home is called a **den**, or lair. Hollow logs, rocky crevices, or gaps in stone walls all make good dens. Small burrows also serve as suitable dens. Weasels often live in burrows, but they are not very good diggers. Instead of making their own, they take over burrows dug by other small animals, such as mice, voles, and chipmunks. Unfortunately, the original owner usually ends up as the weasel's first meal in its new home!

Who Goes There?

All weasels have short legs. When standing on
all fours, their head is just a few inches above the
ground. This can make it difficult to see very far
ahead, especially if they are in tall grass. When a
weasel is hunting, it often stops and sits up on its
hind legs. This way it can use the length of its back
to make itself much taller. Weasels have good
eyesight, sharp hearing, and an acute sense of
smell. In this upright position a weasel can scan
its surroundings for the sight and sound of prey.
It can also sniff the breeze moving over the grass
for the telltale scent of prey or predator.

By standing on its hind legs this weasel has a good view of its prey.

A weasel's coat has
two layers of hair to
keep it warm.

Soft Coats

Weasels have beautiful fur, much like their cousins, the mink. Mink are like big weasels and for centuries people have made coats out of their fur. Weasel fur can be just as silky as mink, but luckily for the weasels, they're too small to be much use in making fur coats.

The fur of weasels is incredibly warm and soft. It feels silky to the touch because it has an outer layer of long, shiny hairs. Those are called guard hairs. Water slides off them. So they help protect the weasel from rain. Underneath the guard hairs is a layer of much shorter hair. That is called underfur. It helps keep the weasel warm.

Winter White

Weasels can be brown. They can also be white.
All weasels **molt**, or shed, their fur in spring and
fall and grow new coats suited to the new season.
In places where it is usually very cold and snowy
in winter, the winter fur is pure white. Being
able to blend in with the surroundings makes it
easier for weasels to sneak up on their prey. It
also makes them less visible to their predators.

In other parts of the world, weasels may stay
brown all year round. In Europe, white ermine
are quite rare, and white ermine fur is considered
very special. The white fur of the ermine with
its black tail was once used to trim the robes of
kings and queens.

Leaving Messages

Weasels can be very smelly animals. The smell comes from a substance called **musk**, which is released by two glands under the weasel's tail. When a weasel relieves itself, it leaves a strong smell of musk on the ground. To people the musk is just an unpleasant smell, but to another weasel it's a message. Every weasel has its own personal smell, and the musk messages it leaves around its **territory** tell other weasels who lives there. Usually the smell warns others to stay away. However, when a female is ready to mate, her smell changes, which serves as a signal to the male weasels that she is ready to mate.

A weasel shows off its white winter coat.

Weasel Weapons

Weasels have teeth that resemble those of a cat or dog. There are two rows of small teeth at the front, with four long teethlike fangs—one on each side of the upper and lower jaw. Along the sides there are some bigger teeth with sharp outer edges. Each of these different sorts of teeth have a different job—but they are all used for catching and eating meat.

The long teeth are called **canines** and a weasel uses them to kill its prey by biting the back of the prey's neck. It's a quick way to do the job. To catch their prey, weasels pounce on it with their front feet. They have five sharp claws on each foot. They use these to hold their prey still so that they can sink their canines into it.

The big sharp-edged side teeth are called **carnassials**. These teeth are used like scissors to slice up meat. The tiny front teeth are called **incisors**. The weasel uses them for nibbling the last bits of meat off the bones.

This weasel's pointed canine teeth are used for killing its victims with a sharp bite.

This weasel is feasting on a small shrew it has just caught.

Tall Order

Weasels eat up to half their own body weight in meat every day. So between dawn and dusk a large adult weasel weighing 12 ounces (360 g) has to find up to 6 ounces (180 g) of food—or six mice weighing at least 1 ounce (30 g) each.

Finding so much food is hard work. The weasel either has to catch several very small animals, such as mice, or one big one to last the whole day. Weasels and ermine are incredibly strong for their size. They often manage to catch animals much bigger than themselves, such as rats or rabbits. They drag the body back to their den or another safe place, so they can eat without the threat of another animal trying to steal their kill.

Storing Food

If a weasel is full and can't eat any more, it will store any leftover food for later. Sometimes the bodies of dead animals are buried in the ground or wedged in a rocky crevice. A weasel may also take them back to its own den and store them in a special "pantry" chamber. A food store like that is called a **cache** (KASH). Weasels build up big caches in the fall. They know fresh meat might be hard to find in winter. As the weather cools the meat chills or even freezes and stays fresh for a long time. Fortunately, weasels don't mind eating frosty meat!

Weasels store food in underground larders for winter when it is hard to hunt.

Male weasels are
aggressive to
rivals when they
are on the scent
of a female.

Meeting to Mate

Weasels usually live alone, but males and females must come together for a short while each year to **mate**. The female leaves smelly scent messages around her territory that tell the local male she is ready to breed. The male comes to visit for a short while and they mate.

The area where a female weasel lives is smaller than the area in which a male weasel roams and hunts. That means there may be other females living in his territory. After he has mated with a female the male moves on straight away to see if he can find another female that is ready to mate. Male weasels have no part in caring for their young.

A Long Wait

Least weasels mate in spring and females give
birth about five weeks later. Least weasels only
live 1 or 2 years. So they have to take their
chances and breed as soon as they can.

Female ermine and long-tailed weasels mate
in summer. But they are pregnant for nearly
ten times as long as least weasels. There is plenty
of food available in summer. That means the
female long-tailed weasels and ermine are very
healthy and strong during the mating season.
Their babies develop inside them slowly. They
don't have their young in winter when food is
scarce. Ermine and long-tailed weasels finally
give birth in spring the following year. If the
long-tailed weasels and ermine babies survive
to become adults, they can live for 6 or 7 years.
So they have time for longer pregnancies than
least weasels.

Baby weasels are born with only a thin layer of fur. Their eyes do not open until they are several weeks old.

37

A litter of baby weasels huddles together in a den for warmth.

Baby Care

Newborn weasels are pink and completely helpless, with almost no fur. It takes a whole month before they will be able to open their eyes. They need a lot of care from their mother and with as many as 12 babies in a **litter**, she is certain to be very busy caring for all her young. She makes a cozy nest lined with the fur from other animals she has caught. She feeds the babies milk for the first month or two of their life. Then she starts to bring them pieces of meat. They grow up fast after that. By about 3 months old the young weasels are usually ready to leave home and survive on their own.

Moving House

Weasel mothers are always anxious about the safety of their young. They never keep them in the same place for very long. A female weasel may have a dozen dens in her territory. She moves her family among them at least every few days. By doing this, the den never builds up a strong smell that might attract other predators to the area.

When planning a move the female first checks out the new den. Then she makes several journeys back and forth, carrying her young one at a time in her mouth. That shows just how gentle she can be: even with all those sharp teeth she manages not to hurt them.

This female weasel
is moving one of her
babies to a new den.

When they are trying to catch rabbits, ermine will sometimes stand on their back legs and sway from side to side.

Deadly Dance

People sometimes see ermine acting very
strangely, running in circles, then pausing
to rear up and weave their body from side to
side. This action seems to be designed to confuse
prey, especially rabbits. People once thought
that this strange dance put the rabbits into
a trance so that the ermine could catch them.
In fact, that might be almost true—the rabbits
get very confused. At first they try to run away,
but the ermine is so quick the rabbit ends up
running in circles. Sometimes it is difficult to
see who is chasing whom. Sometimes the rabbit
escapes, but if the ermine has a chance it will
rush in and kill the rabbit with a quick bite
to the neck.

Pest-control Service

Weasels are very useful animals to have around farms and gardens, because they keep down the number of mice and rats. Sometimes they even come inside buildings in hot pursuit of their prey.

In many ways weasels do a better job than cats do at ridding an area of pesky rodents. They can get into tiny spaces to clear out whole nests of mice. Size for size they eat more than cats because they don't spend as much time just lazing about or dozing in the sun! Weasels don't expect any extra food to be put out for them, they don't bring dead animals into the kitchen, and there are never any veterinarian's fees. How's that for service?

Weasels are
expert killers
of rodents.

45

Ermine like to hide in places where they can easily sneak up on their prey.

Fact and Fiction

There are many traditional stories about weasels. Most tell of their amazing skill as hunters. Native American people considered weasels symbols of good luck. They noticed that weasels were not only very successful hunters, but that weasels themselves were very difficult to catch. They seem to be able to escape all kinds of difficult situations. The saying "to weasel out of something" usually means to get away despite the odds being against you.

Native Americans also thought that seeing a weasel brought good fortune. Catching one was very lucky indeed. If they were skilled enough to catch a weasel, hunters would carry its skin in the hope that some of this good luck would rub off.

Calling all Weasels

Usually weasels never stand still long enough to let you get a good look at them. But if you ever catch sight of one dashing across a path or disappearing into a rocky crevice, you might like to try this neat trick.

Crouch down a few feet from where you saw the weasel disappear. Purse your lips and suck in air to make a squeaky kissing noise. Make two or three squeaks, then wait a few seconds and do it again. To a weasel you'll sound like a frightened mouse or baby rabbit. The weasel won't be able to resist coming to have a look. Keep watching for a curious head to pop up from somewhere nearby. It won't be fooled for long though, so make sure everyone is paying attention!

Words to Know

Burrows   Holes in the ground dug by animals to use as a home.

Cache   A store of food, or the act of storing food by certain animals.

Canines   The long pointed teeth near the front of a mammal's mouth.

Carnassials   Special teeth used for slicing meat.

Den   A weasel's home.

Fossils   The remains of animals or plants that lived long ago and have now turned to stone.

Incisors   The teeth at the very front of a mammal's mouth.

Litter   A group of baby animals born at the same time to one mother.

Mammals	Warm-blooded animals that have hair and feed their young on milk.
Mate	To come together to produce young.
Molt	To shed a coat of fur or feathers and grow a new one at certain times of year.
Musk	A strong scent produced by weasels and some other animals.
Predators	Animals that hunt and eat other animals.
Prey	An animal that is hunted by other animals.
Stoat	Another name for the ermine.
Territory	An area that an animal or group of animals defends as its own private space.

Find Out More

Books

King, C. and R. Powell. *The Natural History of Weasels and Stoats*. New York: Oxford University Press, 2007.

Morgan, S. *The Weasel Family*. Looking At Small Mammals. London: Chrysalis Children's Books, 2004.

Web sites

Long-tailed weasel

animaldiversity.ummz.umich.edu/site/accounts/information/Mustela_frenata.html
Information about the long-tailed weasel. Also has links to other species of weasels and mustelids.

Weasels

www.enchantedlearning.com/subjects/mammals/weasel/Weaselprintout.shtml
Information about weasels with a diagram to print and color in.

Index